WHAT HAPPENS DURING AN EMERGENCY?

Emergency Book for Kids

Children's Reference & Nonfiction

In this book, we're going to talk about what happens when there's an emergency and someone has to go to the emergency room. So, let's get right to it!

Twelve-year-old Mary and her little brother Ted loved to play outdoors together. Ted had just turned five years old and he got a red tricycle for his birthday. He was too small to really ride it the way he wanted to.

He asked his sister Mary to push off on their driveway. They had a steep driveway and that way the tricycle went really fast. It was so much fun for both of them.

One day something bad happened. Mary pushed off at a strange angle and when they came down the hill, the tricycle's wheels turned too early. They both fell off and hit the concrete driveway really hard. Mary had a scraped-up leg, but Ted was really hurt.

He was screaming and crying. He was holding his leg in pain. Mary got up and ran to the house to get help. Her mother raced outside to look at Ted. She was quite upset to see they had both been hurt, but she tried to stay calm. It was time for a trip to the emergency room.

WHAT IS THE ER?

If you need emergency help like Ted did, the emergency room at the hospital or at an urgent care location is the best place for you to get help quickly. The emergency room, which is also known as the ER, is always open because emergencies happen 24 hours, every day.

RGENCY

The doctors, nurses, and staff who work there have seen every type of emergency. They are trained to handle medical issues that require quick action. If you go to a children's hospital, there might be an emergency room that's designed just for children.

GETTING TO THE EMERGENCY ROOM

Your parents or the adult that's taking care of you will need to make a decision when they see how hurt you are. They'll have to decide if they can drive you to the ER themselves or whether to call the emergency number 911 so an ambulance will come to get you quickly.

AMBULANCE

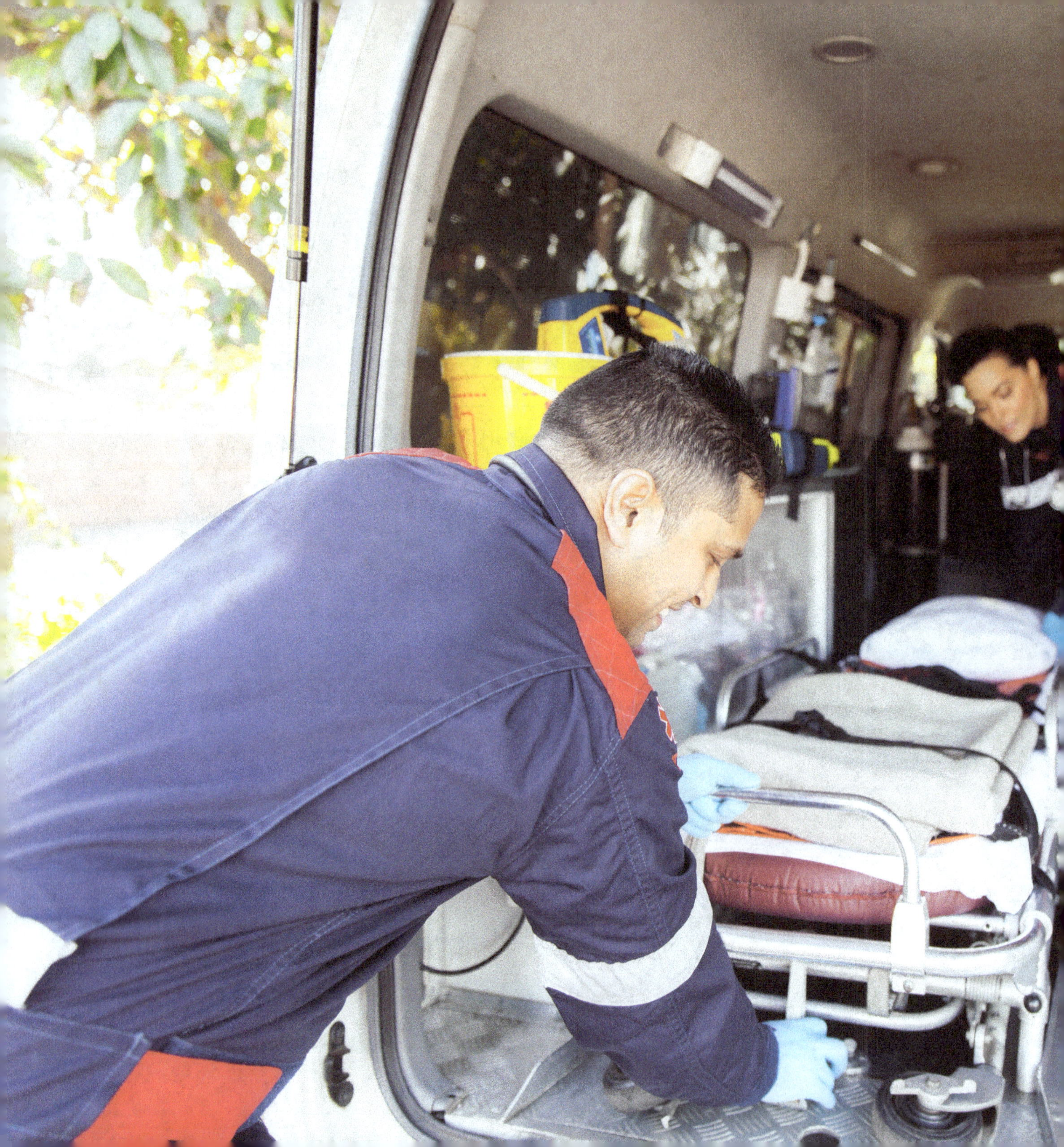

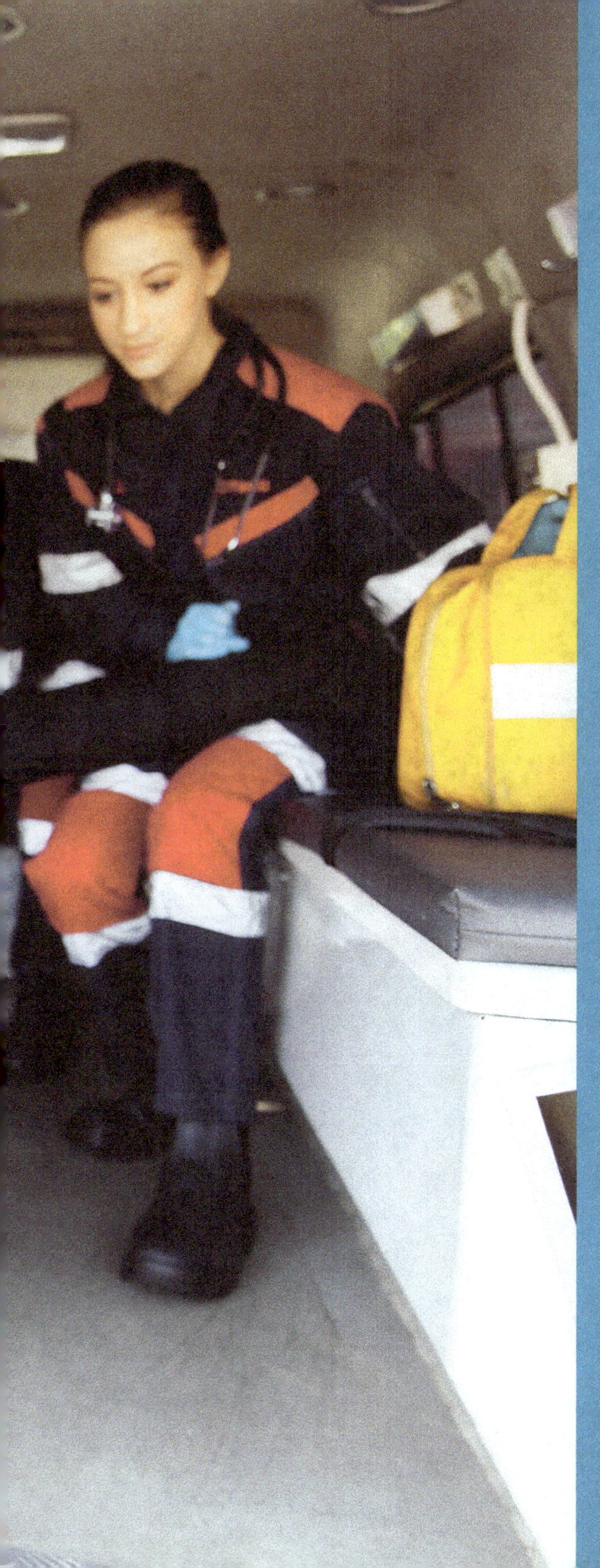

In addition to getting you to the ER quickly, ambulances have other advantages as well. They contain trained medical people who can take care of you until you get to the hospital. Ambulances have very loud sirens so when they transport you to the ER, other cars get out of the way and clear a path.

They're allowed to break the rules when they drive, by driving on the wrong side of the road if necessary to get you to the hospital as quickly as possible. If your parents drove you to the ER, you'll probably see quite a few ambulances parked outside the hospital.

Accident & Emergency
EMERGENCY AMBULANCE
AMBULANCE
KEEP CLEAR

If you're not too injured, while you and your parents are waiting for the ambulance to arrive, they may pack a little bag with a favorite toy or book to take so that you can have something to play with or read before the emergency room doctor sees you.

WHAT HAPPENS WHEN YOU GET THERE?

As soon as you get inside the emergency room, the first thing that your parents or the adult taking care of you will do is check in at the front desk. The staff at the desk will ask you some questions so they can assess how hurt you are and what the nature of the emergency is. If you're really very injured, they will make sure that you get in to see a doctor right away.

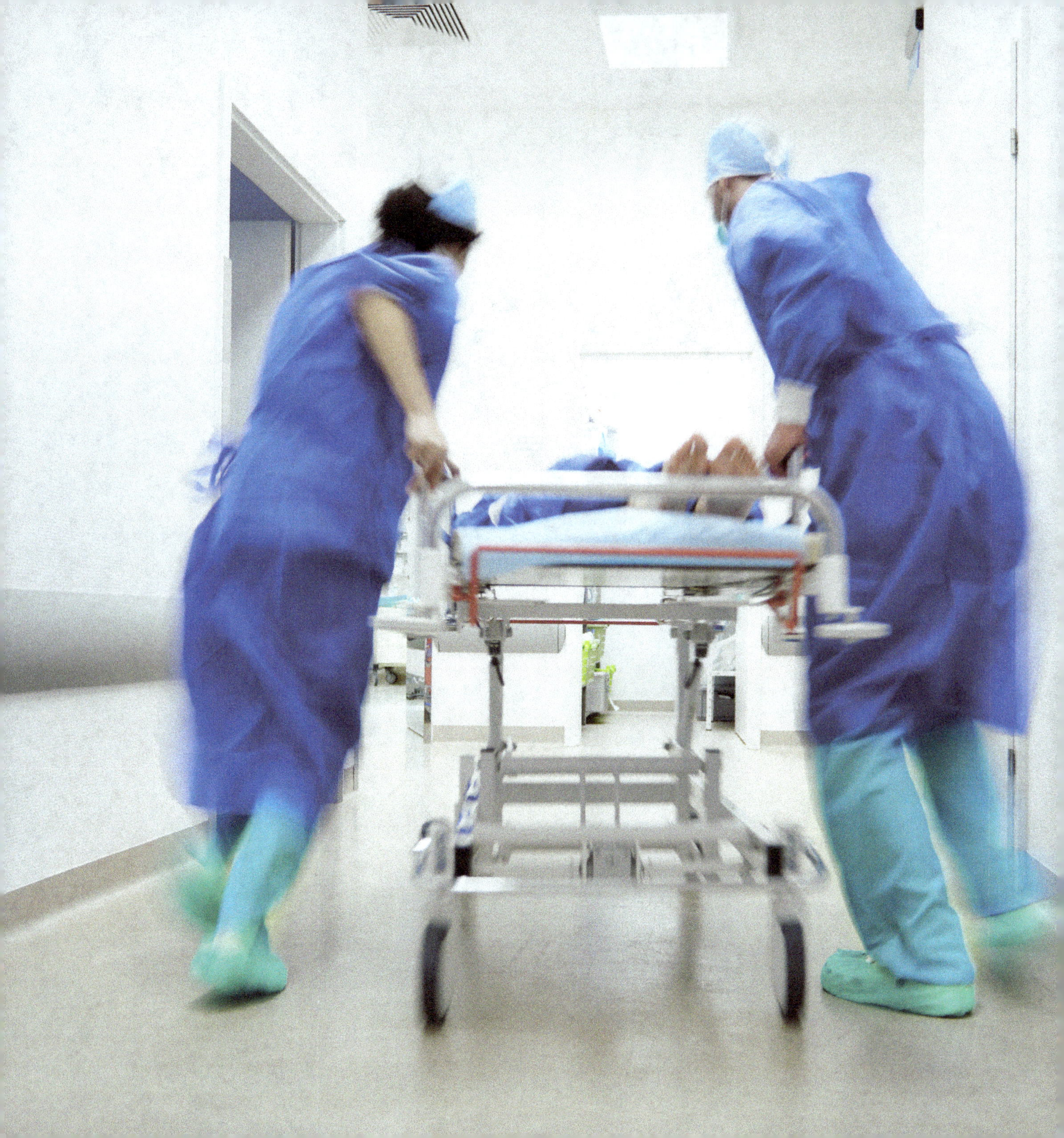

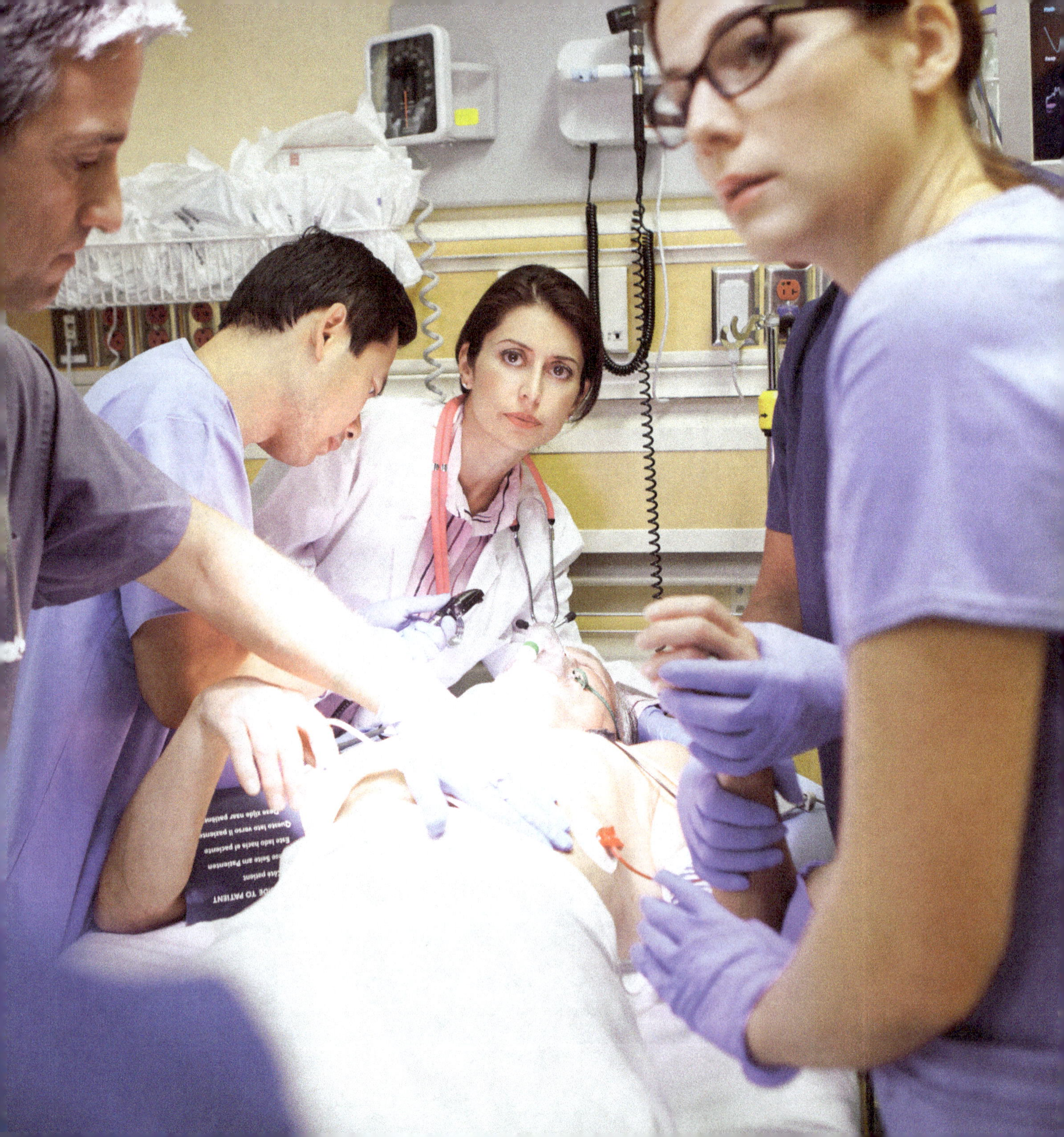
SIDE TO PATIENT
Este lado hacia el paciente
Questo lato verso il paziente
Diese Seite zum Patienten
Deze zijde naar patiënt

If there are other people who are more injured than you are, they may be taken in to see a doctor first. Usually there is a triage nurse there. This type of nurse makes a decision about which patients need to be taken in to see the doctor first.

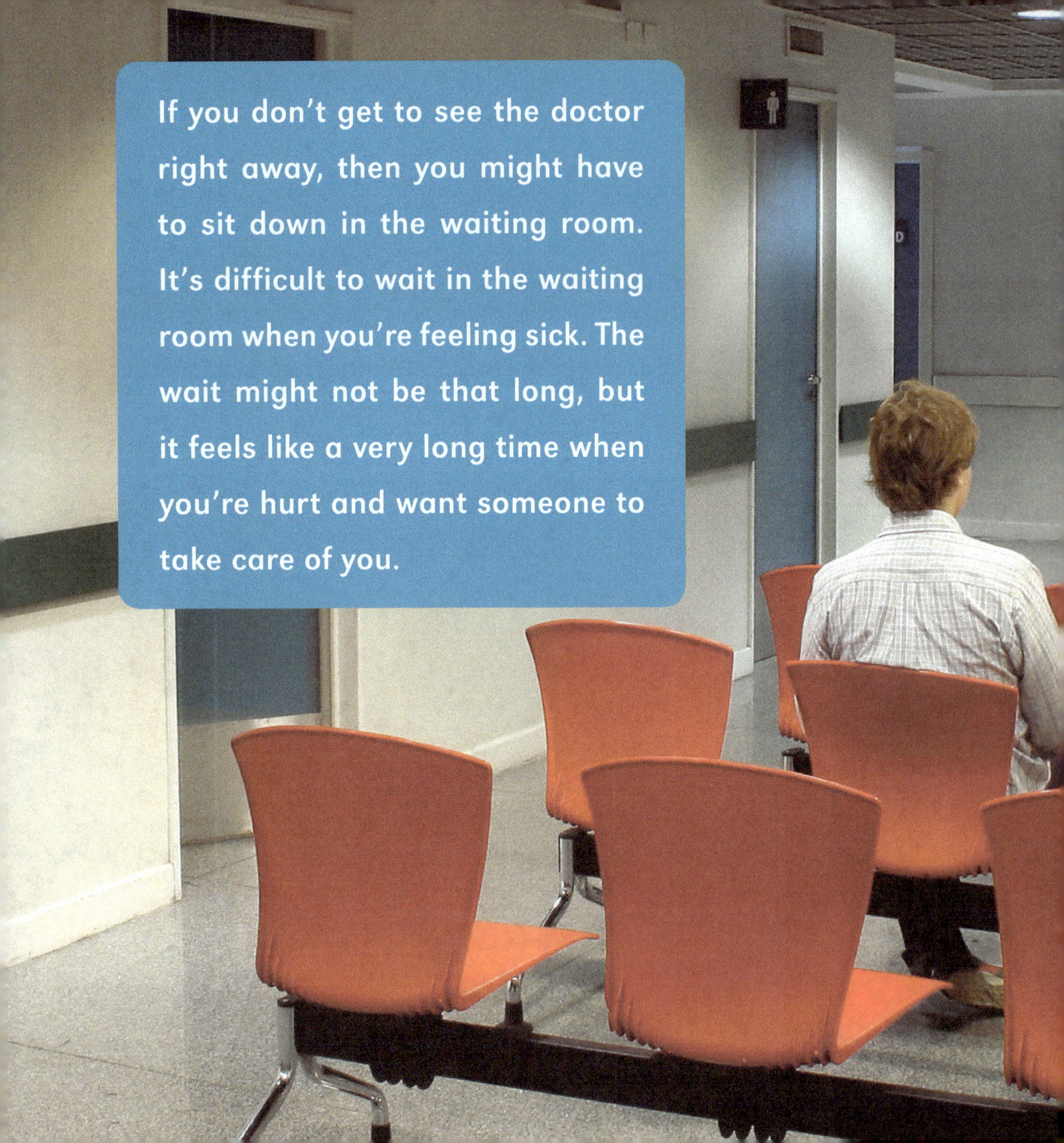

If you don't get to see the doctor right away, then you might have to sit down in the waiting room. It's difficult to wait in the waiting room when you're feeling sick. The wait might not be that long, but it feels like a very long time when you're hurt and want someone to take care of you.

1
Hospital Waiting Room

The waiting room usually has items to distract you and keep you busy, such as toys to play with, magazines or books to read, or a television to watch. When you're not feeling well, sometimes distractions help. Your parents may have brought in a bag with the items they packed from your room. The nurse might tell you not to eat anything or drink anything until you're brought in to see the doctor.

IT'S YOUR TURN TO SEE THE DOCTOR

When it's time for you to see the doctor, a nurse or staff person will call out your name and accompany you to the examining room. You may have to wait there for a while before the doctor comes in to see you. Your dad or mom will be able to stay in the examining room until the doctor gets there.

Examination Room

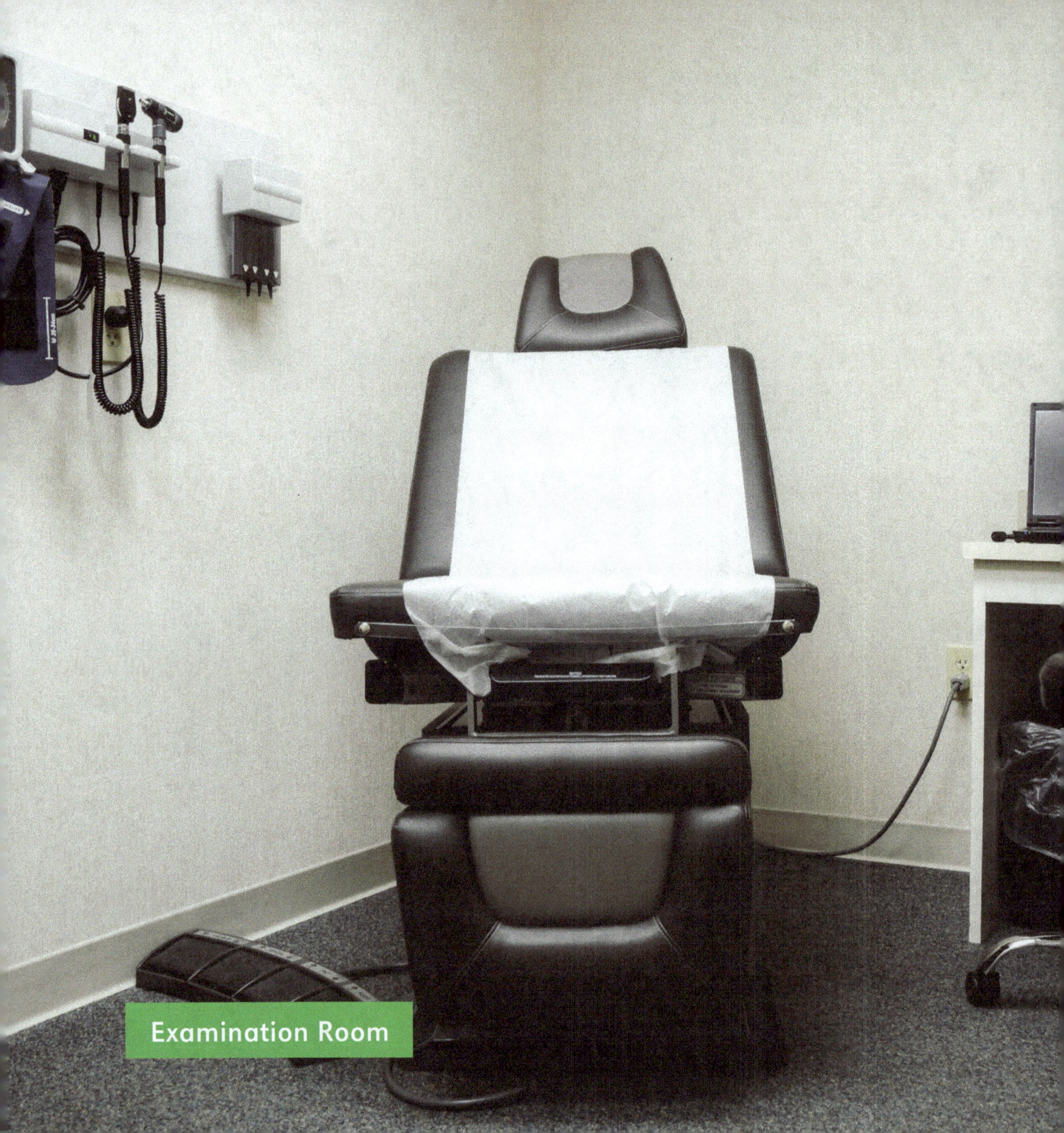

Examination Room

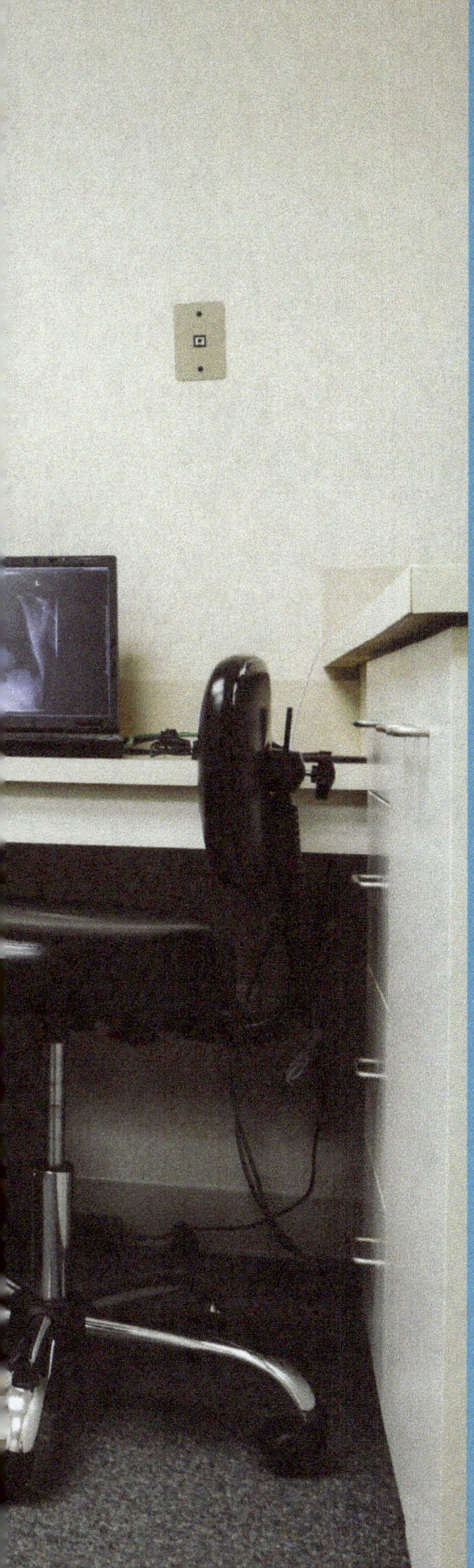

The examination room will have a platform that has a place to lie down and usually several chairs. Sometimes there's a computer in the room for the nurse or doctor to type up notes during your exam. There also might be a monitor that looks something like a TV or computer screen. It might be used to keep watch over your heartbeat or breathing patterns if you're really injured.

You might notice an oxygen tank with some tubing for people who need extra oxygen to breathe. There might be lots of other types of equipment in the room too. The doctor will decide which pieces of equipment you might need. Just because it's there doesn't mean that he or she will use it to examine you or help you.

Oxygen Tank and Regulator Gauges

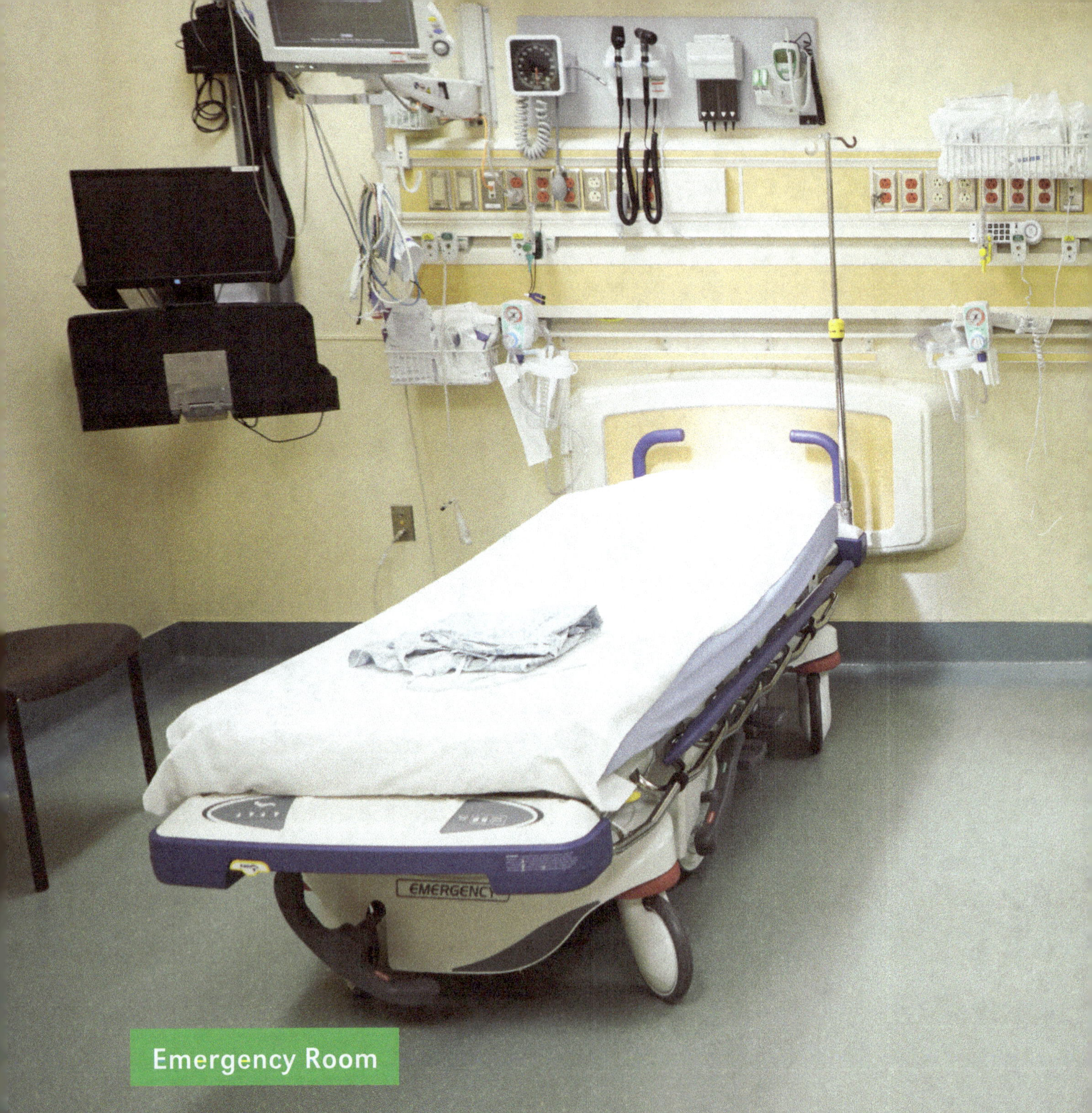
Emergency Room

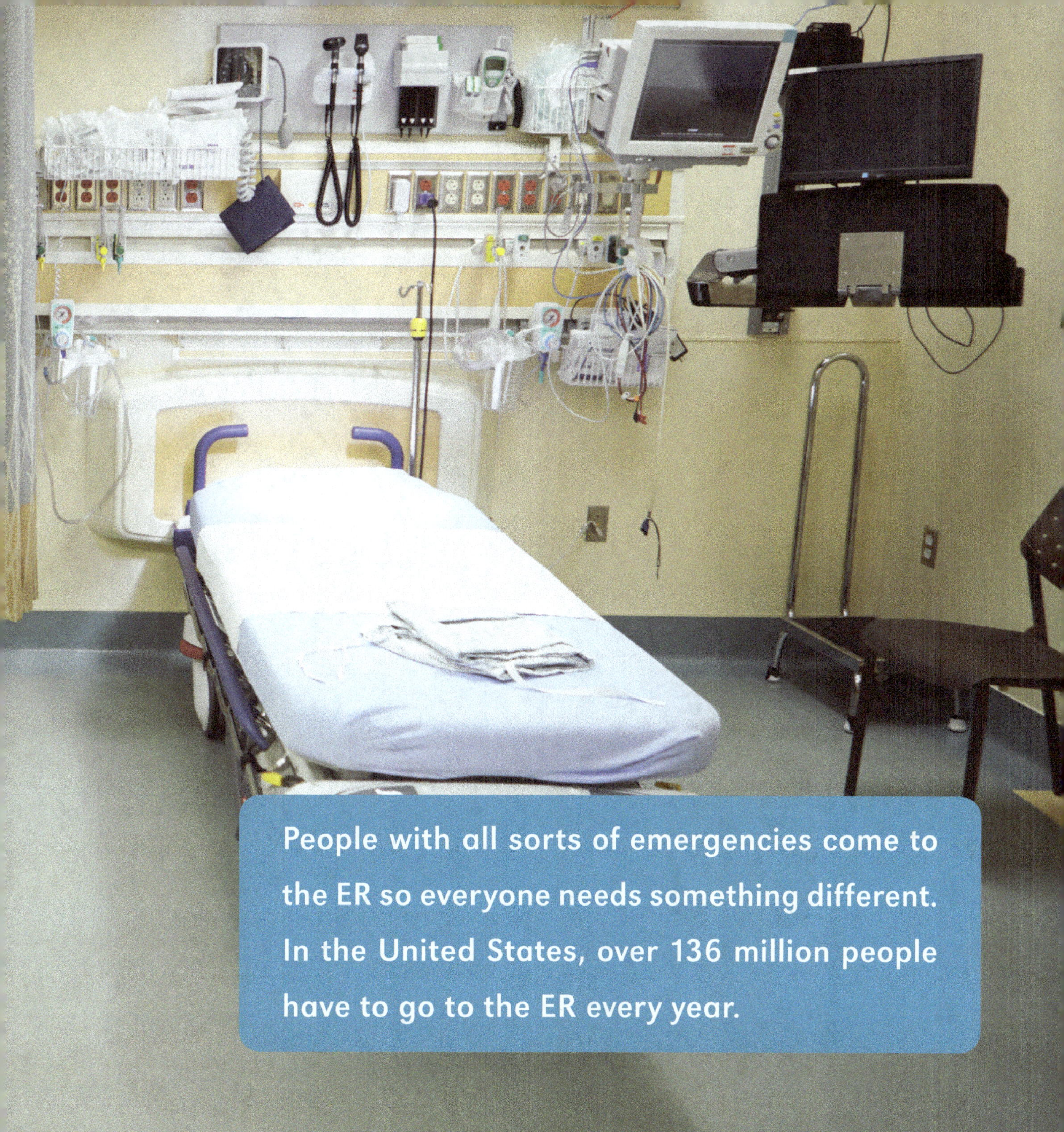

People with all sorts of emergencies come to the ER so everyone needs something different. In the United States, over 136 million people have to go to the ER every year.

Here are some of the most common reasons people go to the ER:

- Chest pains
- Skin infections or unusual rashes
- Cuts and bad bruises, called contusions
- Injuries related to bones or sprains
- Respiratory problems
- Severe toothaches
- Foreign objects in the body
- Back pain
- Severe headaches
- Abdominal pain

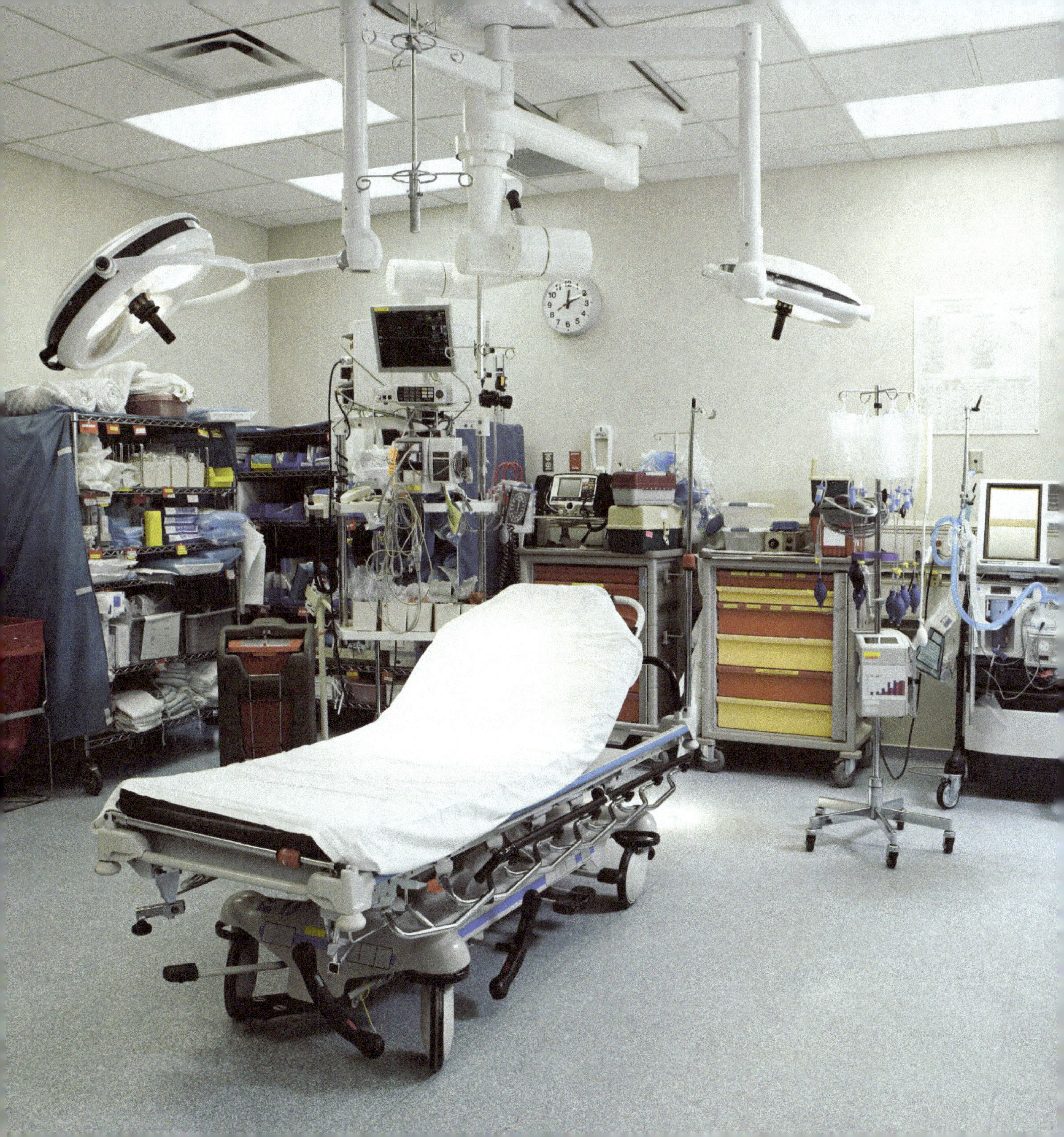

When the doctor comes in, he or she will discuss your situation with your parents. In Ted's case, he broke his leg, so he needed an X-ray. Then, the doctor reset his leg and put a cast on it so it would heal properly. He won't be able to play on his tricycle for a while.

Depending on the injury you have you may need different tests. Sometimes you have to get a blood test. For some injuries you might need a urine test where you pee inside a cup so the doctors have a sample to test. You might need some fluids or liquid medicines fast so the doctor or nurse might use a needle to put an IV in your vein. An IV is an intravenous catheter. It's a very thin tube made of plastic that's placed in your vein.

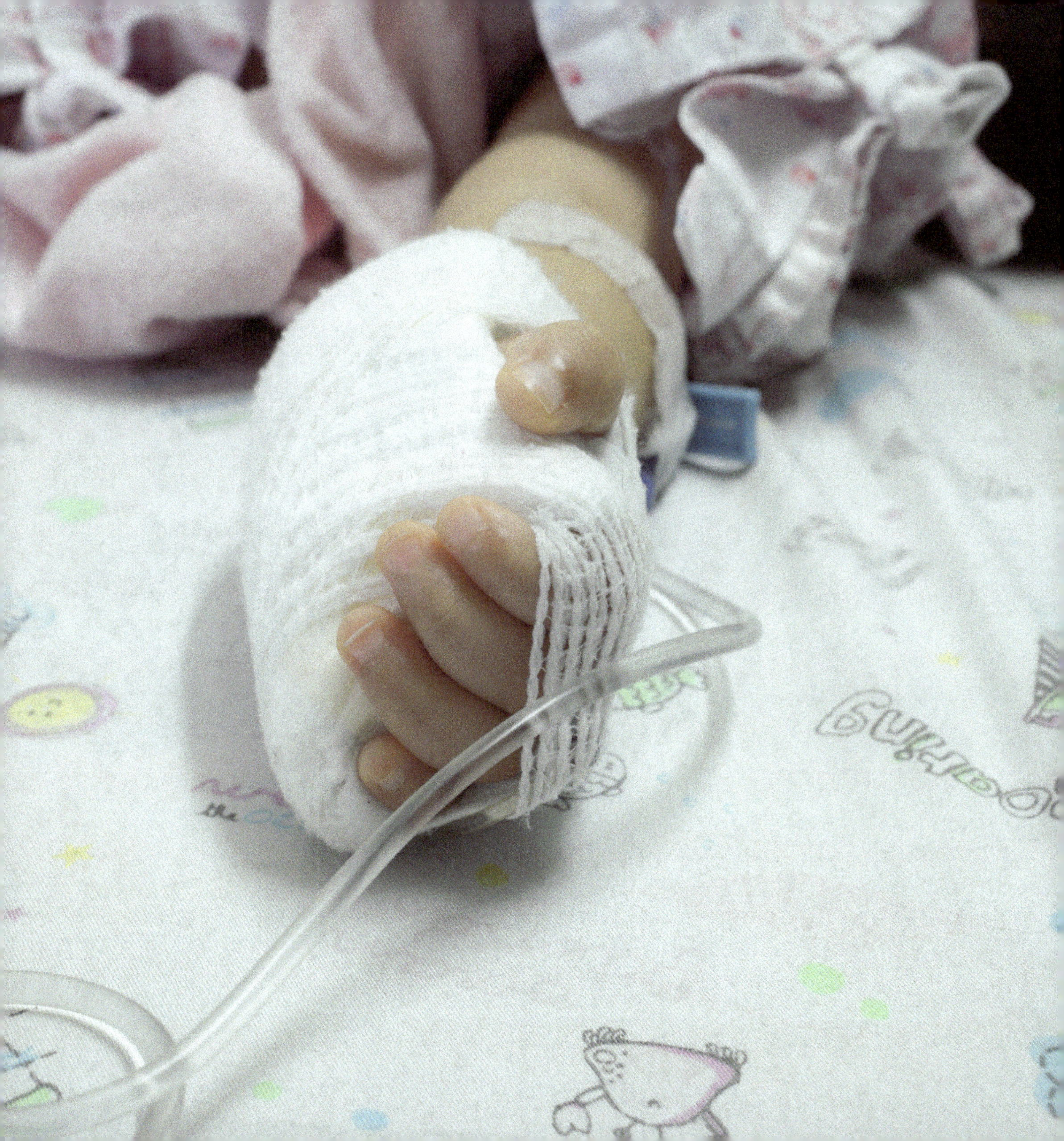

GOING HOME OR GOING TO THE HOSPITAL

After the doctor sees you, he or she will decide whether you can go home after being treated or whether you have to go to the hospital. Most kids end up going home after they are treated at the ER.

The doctor might give you a prescription for some medicine you need to take until you're well. Your parents or the adult who takes care of you can pick up the medicine at the pharmacy.

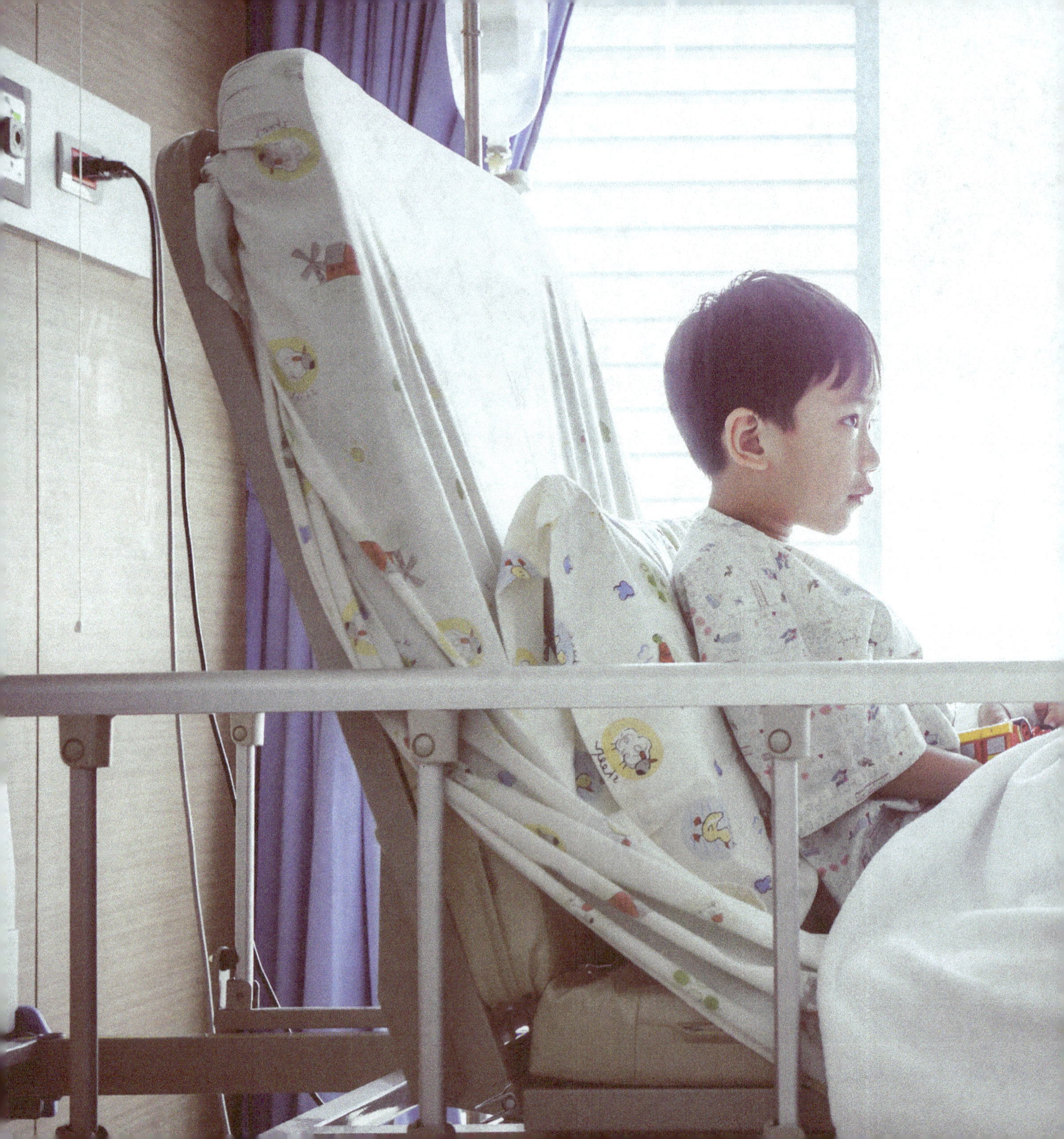

If your injury is serious, the doctor may want you to check into the hospital to say overnight. If you haven't stayed overnight in the hospital before, it may seem kind of scary, but there are trained doctors and nurses who will take care of you. Your mom or dad may be able to stay in the hospital room with you.

Some hospitals have specialists to help injured children. They can help you with the pain or stress you're having and explain things to you with drawings. They can calm you down so you won't feel worried. It's normal to feel worried when you're sick or have an injury.

WHAT HAPPENS AT THE END OF YOUR ER VISIT?

The emergency room doctor will probably suggest that you go back to your regular doctor for a visit. Your parents will set up a follow-up appointment for you. If you had to have stitches or a cast, the doctor will let you know how long it will take before they will be removed.

Ted went home with a cast on his leg and the ER doctor cleaned up Mary's scrape and placed a bandage on it. All the kids in his kindergarten signed Ted's cast and drew pictures on it!

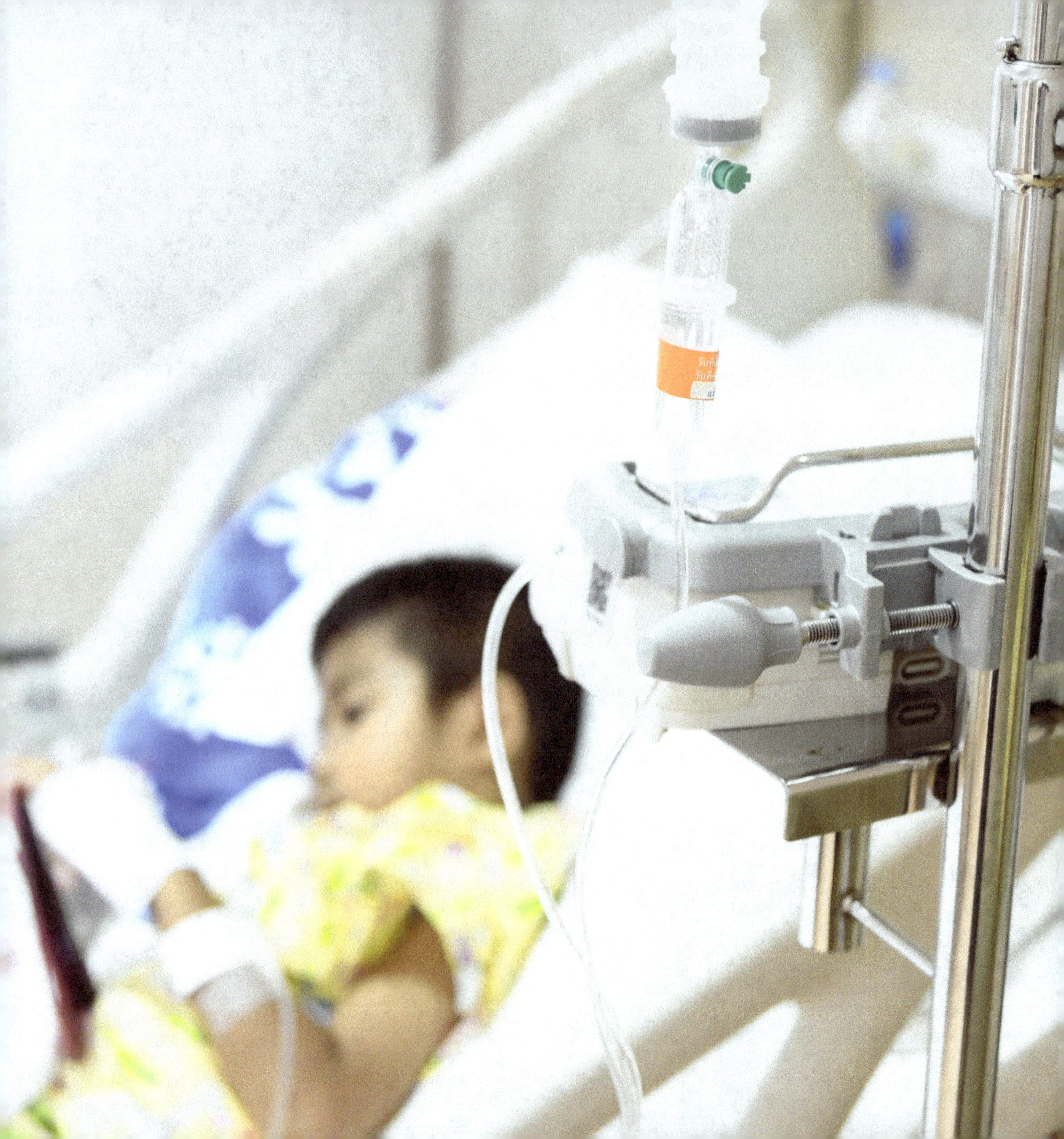

LET'S REVIEW WHAT WE LEARNED!

When you're injured at home or at school, your parents or another adult may drive you to the emergency room at the closest hospital. If you need help on the way, they may call an ambulance to take you there instead. An ambulance has trained medics who can take care of you until you get to the emergency room. When you get to the ER, you may have to wait to see the attending doctor. After the doctor sees you, he or she may run some tests and take care of your injury.

Now that you know more about what happens in a hospital emergency room you may want to read about different types of weather emergencies in the Baby Professor book Chasing Storms and Other Weather Disturbances.

ENCY
E 12'
Emergency

Visit
BABY PROFESSOR
EDUCATION KIDS
www.BabyProfessorBooks.com
to download Free Baby Professor eBooks
and view our catalog of new and exciting
Children's Books